WHAT·DO·WE·KNOW ABOUT 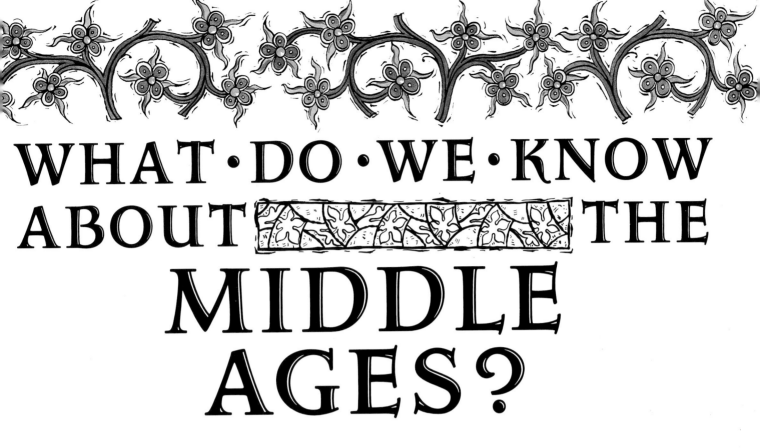 THE MIDDLE AGES?

SARAH HOWARTH

PETER BEDRICK BOOKS

NEW YORK

Published by
PETER BEDRICK BOOKS
2112 Broadway
New York, NY 10023

© Macdonald Young Books Ltd 1995

A CIP catalog record for this book is available
from the Library of Congress,
Washington, D.C. or by request from the publisher.

ISBN 0-87226-384-3

Designer and illustrator: Celia Hart
Commissioning editor: Debbie Fox
Editor: Caroline Arthur
Picture research: Valerie Mulcahy
Series design: David West

Photograph acknowledgements: Front and back cover: Bibliotheque National,
Paris (MS.Fr.599.f.29); John Bethell Photography, pp19(b), 30(t); Bibliotheque
National, Paris, pp31(b) (Latin 8846.f.756v), 36(l) (MS.Fr.12420.f.86), 41(tl)
(MS.Fr.2810/988); Bibliotheque National, Paris/The Bridgeman Art Library,
London, pp12 (Latin 1673.f.103v), 23(t) (MS.Fr.12420.f.71), 24(b) (MS.Fr.616.
f.77), 26(r) (Giraudon) (Latin 18014.f.288v), 27, 40 (Index); Blairs College
Museum Trustees, p37(r); Bodleian Library, Oxford, pp16 (MS.Bod.264.f.82v),
17(br) (MS.Bod.264.f.2v), 20 (MS.Bod.717.f.287v), 21(t) (MS.Bod.264.f.123v),
2 (t) (MS.Bod.264.f.76r), 33(t) (MS.Bod.Douce 374.f.15v); Bolton Museums &
Art Gallery, p18; Bristol Record Office (ref: 01250/1), p9(br); British Library,
London, pp26(l) (Add.42130.f.166v), 30(b) (Cotton.Dom.A.XVII.73v), 35(t)
(Roy.10.E.IV.f.187); British Library, London/The Bridgeman Art Library, London,
pp13(br) (Add.24098.f.25v), 29(t) (Add.29433.f.89), 31(t) (Add.38120.f.8), 32(t)
(Roy.17.F.II.f.283), 33(b) (Add.19720.f.165), 35(b) (Psalter.Roy.2.B.VII.f.78),
39(tl) (Sloan 2435.f.117), 43(t) (MS.16.G.VI.f.404), 43(b) (Luttrell Psalter Add.
42130.f.54); The Dean and Chapter of Chichester, p37(l); Ecole des Beaux Arts,
Paris/Giraudon/The Bridgeman Art Library, London, p17(tl); English Heritage
Photo Library, pp15(t), 42; Fitzwilliam Museum, University of Cambridge, pp13(t)
(MS.242.f.29r detail), 41(br) (MS.165.f.46 detail); Glasgow Museums/The Burrell
Collection, endpapers; Sonia Halliday & Laura Lushington, p29(b); Julia
Hedgecoe, p22; Munich Bayerische Staatsbibliothek, p34; Musée Condé,
Chantilly/Giraudon/The Bridgeman Art Library, London, pp9(bl)
(MS.65/1284.f.3v), 15(b) (MS.65/1284.f.1v); Museo del Patriarca,
Valencia/The Bridgeman Art Library, London, p25(b); National
Gallery, London/The Bridgeman Art Library, London, p8; Sainte-
Foy, Conques/Lauros-Giraudon/The Bridgeman Art Library, London,
36(r); Scala, pp21(b) (Duomo, Pistoia), 28 (Duomo, Siena), 38(r)
(Museo dell'Opera del Duomo, Florence); Trinity College, Cambridge,
pp23(b) (MS.0.9.34.f.7r), 32(b) (0.1.20.f.248v); The Board of Trinity
College, Dublin, p39(r) (TCD.MS.177.f.63r); TRIP, p38(bl); Courtesy
of the Trustees of the V & A Museum, pp14, 19(t), 25(t).

Endpapers: This tapestry was made
in Germany in about 1410; it shows
people haymaking.

Printed and bound in Hong Kong by Wing King Tong Co., Ltd.

99 98 97 9 95 1 2 3 4 5

· CONTENTS ·

WHEN WERE THE MIDDLE AGES?	8
TIMELINE	10
WHERE DID PEOPLE GET THEIR FOOD?	12
WAS THERE ENOUGH TO EAT?	14
WERE MEDIEVAL FAMILIES LIKE OURS?	16
DID MEDIEVAL PEOPLE LIVE IN HOUSES?	18
WHO WENT TO SCHOOL?	20
DID EVERYONE WORK?	22
DID PEOPLE HAVE HOLIDAYS?	24
WHAT DID PEOPLE WEAR?	26
WHAT DID PEOPLE BELIEVE?	28
HOW IMPORTANT WAS RELIGION?	30
DID PEOPLE GO TO THE DOCTOR?	32
WHO RULED THE PEOPLE?	34
WERE THERE MEDIEVAL ARTISTS?	36
WERE THERE SCIENTISTS AND INVENTORS?	38
DID PEOPLE TRAVEL?	40
WHAT WAS LIFE LIKE FOR SOLDIERS?	42
GLOSSARY	44
INDEX	45

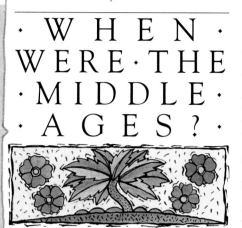

· W H E N · W E R E · T H E · M I D D L E · A G E S ? ·

The 'Middle Ages' is the name given to a period in the history of Europe, between about AD400 and AD1400. After the Roman Empire began to collapse, in about AD400, there was a lot of change. Tribes from Northern Europe moved into the old Roman lands and began to set up new kingdoms. More and more people became Christians. By about 900, life was beginning to settle down. In this book we shall look mostly at this more settled part of the Middle Ages, from about 900 to 1400. We use the word 'medieval' to describe people and things from the Middle Ages.

GOD IN EVERYDAY LIFE

Almost everyone in the Middle Ages believed in God. This picture was painted for King Richard II of England (1367–1400). It shows the king with angels and saints. The angels are wearing King Richard's special badge – a white deer – which was given to his supporters. The painter meant Richard to feel that the angels and saints were his supporters, too.

VILLAINS

We still use some medieval words today, but with different spellings and meanings. In the Middle Ages a 'villein' was one of the poorest peasants, who had no rights or freedom. No one thought much of the villeins. Today a 'villain' means a crook.

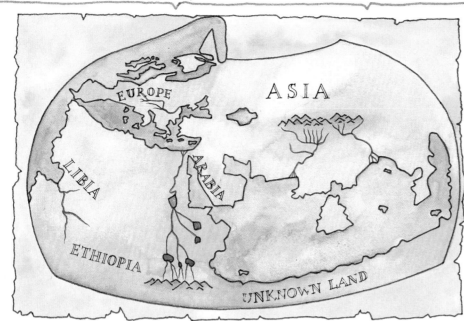

MAP OF THE KNOWN WORLD

The people who lived in Europe in the Middle Ages did not know very much about geography. This map shows what well-educated people in the 15th century thought the world was like. If you compare it with a modern map, you will find some places missing, for example America and Australia. No one in Europe had been to these places, and they did not even know they were there.

FIELDS AND CASTLES

This man is a peasant – a poor farmer. He plows the fields, turning the soil over with a plow pulled by two bullocks. But peasants like this man did not just work to grow food for themselves. They usually had to work for the most important person in the neighborhood. For this peasant, the most important local person would be the man or woman who lived in the castle in the background.

TOWN LAWS

Towns were allowed to make their own laws. This medieval picture shows what could happen when town laws were broken. At the top, people are being thrown into jail. Underneath, bakers are being punished for cheating customers by having moldy bread hung round their necks.

TIMELINE

	900–1000	1000–1100	1100–1200
EVENTS IN EUROPE	**911** Vikings come to live in Normandy (France) from Scandinavia **Carved figurehead from a Viking ship**	**1066** Norman soldiers conquer the Saxons at the Battle of Hastings in England **1086** The Domesday Book is made for William of Normandy, listing the lands he conquered in England **The Domesday Book**	**1147** Lisbon (Portugal) captured from Muslims by Christians
ART AND ARCHITECTURE	First stained-glass windows used in churches First castles built in Europe, in northern France **A scene from the Bayeux Tapestry**	**1070** The Bayeux Tapestry is made, telling the story of the Norman Conquest of England **1093** Durham Cathedral is started, in the Romanesque style	**1135** Cathedral of Saint-Denis in France is started, in the Gothic style **1170–90** Chrétien de Troyes writes poems about King Arthur in French
RELIGION AND LEARNING	**935** The Koran (holy book of the Islamic faith) is written down **A Crusader's helmet and shield**	**1054** Split between two parts of the Christian Church, based in Constantinople and Rome **1095–99** First Christian Crusade against the Muslims in the Holy Land **1098** Cistercian order of monks founded	**1147–8** Second Crusade **1170s** Universities are set up at Salerno (Italy) and Paris **1187** Jerusalem captured by Muslims led by Saladin **1189–98** Third Crusade
EVENTS AROUND THE WORLD	**c.950** Toltecs come to power in Mexico **c.950** Gunpowder invented in China Muslim religion spreads through Egypt, the Middle East, North Africa and Spain	**c.1045** Printing is invented in China Inca Empire grows in Peru **Inca carving**	**c.1150** First Yoruba city states in Nigeria **1150** Angkor Wat, a great Hindu temple, is built in Cambodia **1175** First Muslim Empire is founded in India **1198** Averroës, a great Arab scientist and thinker, dies

1200–1300	1300–1400
1271 Italian traveler Marco Polo arrives in China	**1337** The Hundred Years War begins between England (led by the Black Prince) and France (helped by Joan of Arc)
1284 English kings take control of Wales	
1290 Jews are thrown out of England and Wales	**1347–9** Thousands die of the Black Death all over Europe
1296 England and Scotland go to war over Scottish independence	
	1307–21 Dante Alighieri writes the Divine Comedy, a long religious poem, in Italian
	1339 Kremlin fortress built in Moscow, Russia
	1297–1376 Siena town hall built, Italy
St Francis of Assisi	**1309** The Pope moves from Rome to Avignon in France
1204 Fourth Crusade	**1378** The Church splits, with two popes claiming to lead Christians
1209 St Francis of Assisi starts an order of friars called Franciscans	
1217–21 Fifth Crusade	
1206 The Mongol leader Genghis Khan starts to conquer Asia	**Statue from Benin**
c.1250 First cannons used, in China	
Empire of Mali, in West Africa, grows	**1325** Aztecs build city of Tenochtitlan, Mexico
	1368 Beginning of Ming dynasty, China
	Empire of Benin, Nigeria, grows

A CHANGING SOCIETY

After all the changes that took place in Europe after the end of the Roman Empire, the period from 900 to 1400 was fairly stable. Society was organized in new ways. Kings were powerful, but they needed the support of nobles and knights who would fight for them if someone else tried to take over the country. From about 1000 to 1300, knights were very important as landowners and soldiers.

At the same time, trade and business began to do very well in the towns. Great fairs were set up, where people came to buy and sell goods such as corn, wool and leather. Merchants began to make a lot of money. Although most people lived in tiny villages, towns began to grow. By 1377, 27 towns in England had more than 3000 people.

From about 1000 to 1300 the population of Europe grew steadily. Where there were once huge forests, people cleared away the trees to make room for new farms and villages. Then, in the 1300s, the population fell again, as vast numbers of people died of the plague. This was a disaster, but for the people who stayed alive it meant that life improved. As there were not enough people to do all the work, they could ask for higher wages.

NEW POETRY

Until the 1100s, all books and poems were written in Latin. This was the language used by the Church and all educated people. But from about 1150 onwards, poets such as Chrétien de Troyes in France and Dante Alighieri in Italy started to write in their own national languages. This was harder than it sounds, because until then hardly anything had ever been written down in those languages.

WHERE·DID ·PEOPLE· GET·THEIR ·FOOD?·

For most people, getting food meant hard work – growing it themselves. Peasants had to grow enough food for their families – and enough for their landlords, too. Most peasants paid the rent for their farm plots not in money, but in work and food. They spent many days each year working in their landlord's fields to grow food for him to eat. They also had to give him some of their own produce: some chickens, or some of the honey from their bees. At Easter, they had to give him lots of eggs from their hens. This custom still survives, but nowadays the eggs are chocolate. The system was based on barter and exchanges, rather than money: land was swapped for food and work. Today we call that system the 'feudal system'.

FISH

Dried fish, straight out of the barrel, was a sort of medieval convenience food. There were no refrigerators to keep food fresh, so everything had to be eaten quickly, before it went bad. This meant that most food was eaten where it was grown. But fish and meat could be dried in the open air, smoked or preserved in salt, and then stored and transported in barrels like the one below. Some food was traded over long distances, but it was mostly special food for rich people, such as raisins and spices.

WINE TO DRINK

Here, workers are picking grapes and treading the juice out of them, ready to make wine. Getting a drink was a bit of a problem in the Middle Ages. Water came from wells or streams, because there was no tap water, and tea and coffee were unknown in Europe. Most people drank wine or beer, even children, monks and nuns.

Wooden barrel

Dried fish

HUNTING

Hunting wild animals was a useful way of getting meat for the table. Here you can see a man with a bow and arrow take aim and kill a deer. He is helped by two dogs. All sorts of animals and birds were hunted in the Middle Ages, from deer and rabbits to herons and small birds. But only wealthy people ate much meat.

Pitchfork

Sickle

Wooden rake

THE WORK FORCE

The picture on the right shows peasants taking a break in the fields at harvest time. Men, women and children all worked together. Horses and oxen pulled carts full of all sorts of loads, such as hay. Oxen were also used to draw the plow. But people had to do all the other jobs with their own hands. Corn or hay was cut with a sharp knife called a sickle, and then turned over to dry with rakes and pitchforks.

THE FARMING YEAR

Autumn – threshing corn, plowing fields, cutting trees for firewood, killing animals for meat, gathering nuts

Winter – harrowing fields, planting wheat, mending tools, cleaning ditches

Spring – planting oats and barley, lambing

Summer – hay-making, harvesting crops, shearing sheep, collecting honey from bees

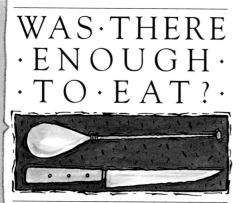

WAS·THERE ·ENOUGH· ·TO·EAT?

In the Middle Ages, what you had to eat depended on who you were. Wealthy people, like kings and queens and knights and their ladies, had more than enough to eat. They had a wider choice of food than ordinary people. Poor people often went hungry. If the harvest was bad, they might even die of starvation. By modern standards, even the people who ate well had an odd diet. Food was sprinkled with lots of fiery spices, to make quite sure that if it was going bad no one would notice. Fruit and vegetables were rarely eaten raw: medieval cooks thought this was positively unhealthy.

PIG-STICKING

Most country people kept a pig and a few animals. They lived almost as part of the family, usually in one end of the house. But there wasn't enough food for the family unless the pig was killed. So in the end it was time to become a butcher and add some bacon to the family's winter stock of food.

Buttered Worts
Take all manner of good herbs that you may get, and put them on the fire with fair water. Put thereto clarified butter a great quantity. When they are boiled enough, salt them; let no oatmeal come therein. Dice bread small in dishes, and pour on the worts and serve them forth.

A PEASANT'S MEAL

For poor people, meals were always much the same: eggs, bread, porridge, cabbage, bacon and onions. Sometimes the eggs and bacon ran out and meals were even more boring. Almost everything was home-made or home-grown. This recipe uses lots of herbs and plants, or 'worts' as they were called. These included borage (a type of leafy plant), nettles and cabbage. With most meals people drank ale, which was brewed locally. A woman known as the 'ale-wife' was usually in charge of this work. If the peasants could get enough food, it was quite a healthy diet. There were few sweet things, which nowadays cause tooth decay and health problems. Medieval people used honey as a sweetener.

GIVING TO THE CHURCH

The peasants had to give one tenth of their crops to the Church. This huge barn was built to store the produce given to one group of monks in England. Few Church officials went hungry.

A BANQUET FOR HENRY IV

When King Henry IV of England sat down to dinner on the day he was crowned in 1399, there were all creatures great and small on the menu: boar's head and tusks, young swan, pheasant, heron, venison, crane, partridge, quail, rabbit, small birds, peacock and egret. In between the meat dishes, the guests found room for sweet dishes such as quinces in sugar, custards and cooked apple.

TABLE MANNERS

Jug

Cup

The picture on the right shows a nobleman's banquet taking place with great ceremony in the 1400s. You can see all the dishes of food on the table. Table manners were very important on occasions like this, but medieval manners were different from ours. People did not eat from plates or bowls, but from a hunk of bread. Each serving was shared between two people, who politely spooned bits up for their partner. At the end of the meal, the old bits of bread were given to the poor and hungry people waiting outside.

·WERE· MEDIEVAL ·FAMILIES· LIKE·OURS?

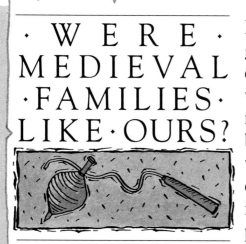

In the Middle Ages, many people lived in big family groups. Grandparents, aunts, uncles, parents and several children might all live under one roof – especially in wealthy families. In the houses of knights and noblemen, the number of people was even bigger, because of all the servants, friends, guards and soldiers who had to be included. There were always visitors coming and going, too. People believed that it was very important to look after anyone who came to stay, and all passing travelers, even strangers, could be sure of a welcome. Some visitors stayed for years. The children of knights and nobles, for example, were sent away from home when they were quite young to grow up in the houses of their parents' friends.

LEARNING TO FIGHT

Parents expected their children to grow up fast, and treated them like little adults. The sons of noble families had to learn to become knights. At about the age of ten they started training, which meant practicing how to ride and use weapons. The boy here is riding a horse on wheels and trying to hit a target with a weapon called a lance.

 A MEDIEVAL FATHER

To people in the Middle Ages, the idea of helping your parents was very important. Children didn't stop doing what their parents wanted when they started to grow up. In fact, many people felt that this was when their children should start to give something back for all their parents' hard work. An English knight called John Paston put it like this: 'Every man that has brought his children up to the age of 12 years then expects to be helped and profited by his children.' John Paston was probably hoping that his children would make friends with important people, or marry someone rich. Children were supposed to marry the people chosen by their parents, whether they liked them or not.

TOYS

Children in the Middle Ages had plenty of fun and games. Their toys included hobby horses, like the one here, hoops, dolls and spinning tops. In poor families, these would probably have been home-made.

Hobby horse

The children of knights and nobles were more likely to have toys that were bought at a fair, or from a toymaker in town.

WORKING CHILDREN

The children of peasants and other working people, such as craft-workers, had to help their parents grow food or make money for the family. In this workshop, a carpenter's family is hard at work – even the little boy is collecting up wood-shavings to keep the shop clean and tidy. In towns, some children were sent away from home to learn a trade at about the age of ten. They worked as 'apprentices' (trainees) and learned about the business from an adult craftsman. Tailors, goldsmiths, apothecaries (doctors), carpenters and other craft-workers all took on child apprentices. The apprenticeship lasted for about seven years.

BEING BORN

The picture on the right shows a baby being born in an important family. Having a baby was dangerous for women in medieval times. Because nobody really understood about keeping properly clean or about the ways a woman having a baby can become sick, many women died giving birth. Being born was also risky for babies. Many babies died from infections in the first days or weeks of life. This meant that although it was normal for women to become pregnant many times, not all of their babies survived. Out of every ten babies who were born, as many as five might die before they grew up.

Babies in a carrying basket

LOOKING AFTER CHILDREN

After they were born, babies were swaddled (wrapped up tightly), as you can see here. They couldn't move around at all. Medieval parents were very strict and expected their children to obey them. Children who didn't do what their parents wanted were often whipped. There is no evidence about what medieval children thought.

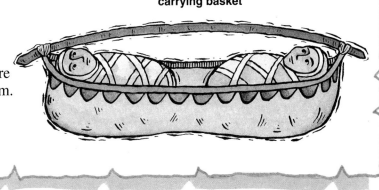

· D I D · MEDIEVAL · PEOPLE · · LIVE · IN · HOUSES ?

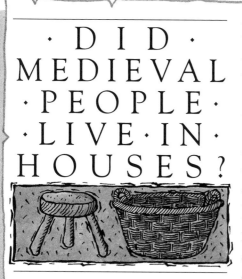

People lived in all sorts of different places in the Middle Ages. Peasants lived in small cottages, with only one or two rooms. Knights and important people lived in castles, which as well as being homes were also fortified buildings made for war, with towers, thick walls and good defenses. In the towns there were houses and workshops for merchants and craft-workers. Monks and nuns lived in monasteries and nunneries, special groups of buildings that included places to sleep, eat, study and pray.

Keys

GREAT HALL

This was the great hall at Smithills, in Lancashire, the home of a wealthy English knight in the 1300s. This room was the center of family life. Meals were eaten here, the servants came here to collect their wages, and the women spent their day here sewing, making clothes and using the spinning wheel. Rushes were spread on the floor for warmth, and wooden shutters kept out the wind. For a medieval knight this was the height of luxury.

FIXTURES AND FITTINGS

Even wealthy people had only a small number of belongings. In 1474, a knight called Sir Thomas Stonor thought these things were important enough to go on the list of his furniture: fire irons, sheets, blankets, a feather bed, two frying pans, an axe for chopping wood and two tapestry cushions.

PEASANTS' HOVELS

These run-down cottages would have belonged to poor peasants. Because they were made with thatched roofs and rough walls of mud and sticks, peasants' cottages needed repairs all the time to make them dry and weatherproof. A lot of the time they were damp, dark, smelly and miserable, with only small holes for windows.

FURNITURE

Below are a baby's cradle and a chest from a wealthy household. A chest was a wardrobe, safe and cupboard all rolled into one. The lady who kept the keys to the chest was a very important person.

Baby's cradle

Wooden chest

TOWN HOUSE

Town houses, like this one, were a bit more comfortable than the peasants' cottages. They had more than one story, and were cozily furnished inside, with colorfully painted walls and rugs on the floor. If you look carefully, you can see that this house was built with a timber frame, which gives it its shape. The areas between the timber frames were filled in with plaster, which was then painted.

UNWELCOME VISITORS

Rats could be found in even the best-kept medieval houses. Medieval housekeepers had no inside water supply, no bathrooms and no refuse collection. It was hard to keep houses clean. This was dangerous, because rats carried germs and spread diseases.

Rats

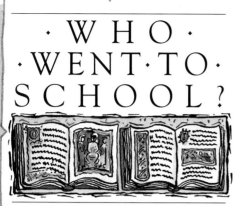

· W H O · W E N T · T O · S C H O O L ?

During the Middle Ages, lots of schools were set up, but not everyone was allowed to go to them. Most schools were only for boys. Many schools were run by the Church in monasteries or cathedrals. Here, boys were taught in the Latin language. All Christian books and prayers were in Latin, so this training meant boys could take part in church services and read the Bible. The boys who went to these schools were expected to become monks or priests themselves when they were old enough. Schools were also set up in towns for boys who were going to be merchants.

WRITING TOOLS

Pens were usually made from bird feathers with the thick end cut into a 'v', or they could be made of metal. The pointed end was dipped in a pot of ink. There were many different recipes for making ink, including boiling up tree bark. Until the mid-1200s, paper was unknown in Europe, and parchment was used for writing on. It was made from animal skin and had to be scraped with a sharp knife to make it ready for use. A stylus could be used to write on soft wax.

Metal pen

Stylus

Ink pot

WRITING BOOKS

Above is a medieval picture showing how books were made: by hand. Every new copy of a book had to be carefully written out, word by word. This work was done by monks, like the one above. They were famous for the beautiful books they produced. The monks usually worked on religious books, such as copies of the Bible and stories about the saints. One monk in Britain, called Bede (673–735), wrote about 80 books, nearly three a year.

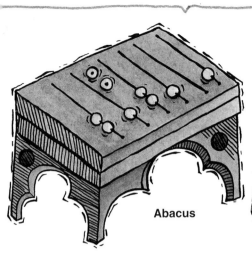

Abacus

SEAL

Seals were special wax stamps, which were fixed to letters and important papers to prove they were not forgeries. Only well-to-do people used seals. Every person's seal was different, so the seal showed who had sent the letter. Because many people could not write their name, they used a seal instead of a signature.

Seal

CLASSROOM

Here you can see a teacher (sitting in a chair) about to cane one of his pupils for bad behavior. The other pupils are meant to be hard at work, probably learning passages from their books by heart. All the pupils here are boys.

ABACUS

This is an abacus – a medieval adding machine. The abacus was divided into columns: one for units (numbers up to ten), one for tens, one for hundreds and so on. Counters were put in the columns to show different numbers. For 105, for example, a counter went in the hundreds column and five counters went in the units column.

UNIVERSITIES

The picture below shows students at a medieval university listening to a teacher and taking notes. The first universities were set up in Italy and France in the 11th and 12th centuries. Some became famous for teaching particular subjects, such as law and medicine. All lectures were given in Latin, and universities were only open to men who had done some religious training.

WHAT ABOUT GIRLS?

Most girls didn't go to school – instead, they learned housekeeping. A 14th-century book includes this conversation between a servant girl and her mistress, which shows what girls were expected to do: 'I am making the beds, shaking the cushions on benches and stools: I am cleaning the solar (sitting room), the chamber (bedroom), the house and the kitchen,' says the servant girl. 'Come down! Bring towels, linen and coal. Blow the fire until it flares. Boil the pots. Fry some fat, lay the table and bring the long cloth. Put water in the hand basins,' orders the mistress.

In the Middle Ages, ideas about work were different from ours. Work didn't mean doing a particular job to earn money. Most people worked, but the work that they did depended on who they were. Knights worked by fighting for the king or queen, who gave them land and let them keep captured treasure. Women worked by looking after the home and family. Peasants grew food, in return for land and a house. Monks, nuns and other religious people worked by praying and serving God, and people gave them gifts. None of these people were actually paid. Merchants and craftsmen, who worked for money, were the odd ones out.

STONEMASON

This mason is shaping a piece of stone using a hammer. Masons worked on big buildings such as castles and cathedrals, moving on when the work was finished. They spent five to seven years learning their trade, and were paid 4d (four pennies) a day.

MONEY

Money was important to merchants, traders and craftsmen, who bought and sold goods. But in the countryside people often used to swap or 'barter' goods – a catch of fish in exchange for help in the fields, for example.

Coins

WHAT COULD YOU BUY WITH YOUR MONEY?

A table and two benches	4s 6d
A grey horse	£3
2 silver cups	£2 11s 8d
A dovecote (bird roost)	6s 8d
2 boxes of sweetmeats	10d
2 geese	10d
3 pigs	12½d

£1 = 20 shillings ; 1 shilling = 12 pence (d)
£1 = about $1.60 US in 1995

Prices did not stay the same all the time; they sometimes went up. One thing is certain: peasants, who earned 1d (a penny) a day for haymaking in the 1300s, would have had trouble affording any of these things. Knights, ladies and nobles had more money to spend.

MERCHANTS

Merchants and craftsmen worked by buying and selling goods. In towns, painted signs hung outside each shop to tell people who worked there: scissors at the cloth shop, a pestle and mortar at the pharmacy. Groups of traders formed into clubs called guilds, which made rules about business and fixed prices. Guilds arranged feasts and religious services, too. One English guild took St Anthony as its patron and used St Anthony's special emblem, a pig with a cross, which you can see below.

SPINNING AND WEAVING

Even ladies from noble families worked to keep the household fed and clothed. Here, women from a noble household make woolen cloth. The two women at the front are carding the wool – combing it smooth to make it ready to spin. The lady in red uses a pole called a distaff to spin the wool into thread, and then the lady in blue weaves the thread into cloth on a loom.

Guild emblem

KNIGHTS

Knights in England had to serve the king for 40 days a year without pay, or two months a year in wartime. Most of this time was spent guarding the king's castles, or training for battle. Here, two knights, both in armor, fight on horseback. Fighting competitions, called tournaments, were held all over Europe. The knight who knocked his opponent off his horse was the winner.

DID·PEOPLE ·HAVE· HOLIDAYS?

The word 'holiday' was invented in the Middle Ages. But at that time, it meant a holy day – a day with special religious importance, when work stopped. Holy days took place at fixed times each year. For example, Christmas and Easter were the most important holy days, when people had a week off. There were many other holy days, too, which added to people's leisure time. People found all sorts of different ways to spend their free time. Singing and dancing were always fun. Games, sports, hunting and feasting were popular, too.

DANCING BEAR

Here, the trainer is playing a tune while the bear dances. Many entertainers like this wandered from place to place, sure of a warm welcome wherever they went. Fairs always had a carnival atmosphere, with jugglers, puppeteers and magicians turning up to charm the crowds. Wandering singers and musicians, known as troubadours, were especially welcome by the castle fireside on a dark winter's night.

HUNTING

Many wealthy medieval people were as fond of hunting animals as people today are about sports like football. It wasn't only men who went out hunting – women enjoyed it, too. There were many different ways of hunting. The two noblemen on the right are hunting deer on horseback. They might also go hawking, which meant releasing specially trained birds of prey to catch smaller birds, such as duck, as they flew along. The hawks' owners would argue endlessly about whose bird was best.

MAY DAY

May 1, May Day, was the start of summer, and there were all sorts of special celebrations to enjoy. Before dawn, people went out to the woods and fields to pick flowers and cut branches of green leaves and blossom to decorate their homes. Songs, dances and games followed. Here, you can see the flowers and greenery being brought home.

CHRISTMAS

Christmas was the longest holiday of the year. It stretched from Christmas Eve (24 December) to Epiphany (6 January). In church, people celebrated the birth of Jesus Christ. At home, they put up green leaves, such as holly and ivy, and burned a huge Yule log on the fire. Rich people gave each other gifts. But the most important part of the holiday was having fun. Even the Church joined in, and on 1 January priests played the fool in church.

MUSIC

Many different types of music were popular. In church, monks and nuns chanted hymns and psalms. In everyday life, people liked love songs and songs with rowdy choruses. In the 1100s wandering scholars known as goliards were especially famous for their drinking songs. Popular musical instruments included harps, trumpets, organs, bagpipes, lutes, pipes, drums and hurdy-gurdies.

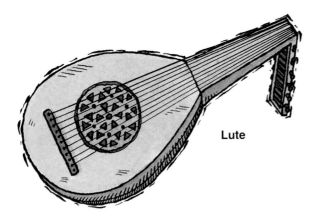

Lute

Pipe

GOLF

The picture on the right shows a game of golf in progress. Golf was first played in the Middle Ages. Another game that began at this time was soccer. It was very popular with apprentices in London, who played it in the city streets and annoyed passers-by.

·WHAT·DID· PEOPLE ·WEAR?·

Many different styles of clothing were worn in the Middle Ages. Poor people needed to keep warm and be able to work, so they had simple clothes. Knights and nobles, on the other hand, wore costumes in expensive materials and bright colors. For these people fashions changed – during the Middle Ages, rich people's clothes became more and more elaborate and less and less practical. But for peasants and working folk, clothes were home-made, dyed in drab colors and frequently patched and mended. One outfit might last a poor person for many years.

PEASANT WOMAN
Peasants dressed in grays, dull reds and other dark shades. Women wore a rough sleeveless tunic over a dress with sleeves. A hood was wound round the head for warmth.

RICH MEN'S CLOTHES
These nobles are dressed in the height of fashion of the 1400s. The pink tunic has long, trailing sleeves cut in a jagged pattern. This type of tunic was called a *houppelande*. On his head, this man wears a hood of the same basic design as the one worn by the peasant woman, but in elegant, expensive cloth.

26

WORKING CLOTHES

People's work and way of life had a big effect on what they wore. For working people like these masons, clothes had to be very practical. They wore a tunic that came down to mid-thigh over a pair of leggings, or 'hose'. The leggings could be rolled down in hot weather, as you can see here. They had no special clothing to protect them when they were doing dangerous jobs. Workers wore clothes made of rough woolen material. Only knights and nobles were allowed to wear silks or velvets.

Fashionable head-dress

Ivory comb

Buckles

WOMEN AND FASHION

Wealthy women could afford to be stylish. Ornate buckles and ivory combs like these were all part of their wardrobe. Head-dresses became very elaborate. One popular style was cone-shaped, and another was like a pair of horns. It was fashionable for hair to be tucked completely out of sight. Sometimes women added to this look by shaving the hair from their foreheads and eyebrows.

KEEPING CLEAN

Keeping clean was not easy in the Middle Ages, when houses didn't have running water or bathrooms. In castles and the homes of the rich, a page boy brought a jug of hot water and bowl to the bedrooms each morning for people to wash. Soap could be made at home by boiling up animal fat and wood ash, but rich people would buy expensive perfumed soap, too. All the same, keeping clean was not a top priority with medieval people. Wearing rough, dirty clothes was even supposed to show that a person was particularly religious, and hermits sometimes wore hedgehog skins or other harsh clothes next to the skin. Fleas and lice spread easily in conditions like these. A French monk called Abelard made this suggestion for nuns: 'To stop vermin getting into the clothes and allow dirt to be washed away, the nuns should have two sets of clothes' – one to wear and one to wash.

27

WHAT·DID ·PEOPLE· BELIEVE?

Nearly everyone in Europe in the Middle Ages was a Christian. Prayers were part of people's everyday lives, and people believed that everything they did would be punished or rewarded by God. The local priest was often one of the most important people in a village. The Church was so powerful that its leaders helped kings and queens to rule their countries. It was also very wealthy, because people gave gifts to their local cathedral or monastery to show how much they believed in God. Although most people were Christians, in parts of Spain and Portugal there were many Muslims. Many Jewish people lived in Europe, too. Jews and Muslims were often attacked by Christians for their beliefs.

PREACHING TO THE PEOPLE
This picture shows a famous friar, St Bernardino (1380–1444), preaching to people in Italy to teach them about Christianity. Bernardino drew big crowds of eager listeners. One pope described him as 'the best teacher of all'. Sermons like Bernardino's were especially important because church services were in Latin, which only educated people could understand.

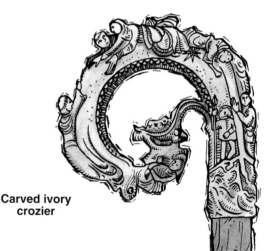

Carved ivory crozier

BISHOPS
A bishop was the Christian leader of one area of the country, known as a diocese. His job was to look after all the Christian people in the diocese. To show this, he carried a special pole like a shepherd's crook, called a crozier.

STAINED GLASS
This stained-glass window shows Jesus Christ as a child with his mother, the Virgin Mary. Pictures were an important way of teaching ordinary people, who couldn't read, about their religion.

Church decorations

PUNISHMENT
Paintings like this one, showing demons carrying sinners off to punishment, were in many churches. Christians believed that people who led bad lives would go to hell when they died – even kings and nobles. It was especially important to obey all the teachings of the Church and not make up your own ideas about God. People who did this were called heretics, and were punished by the Church.

Lead pilgrim badge of St Thomas Becket

PILGRIMAGE
Going on a pilgrimage to the tomb of a saint was a special way to show your love of God. Many sick people went on pilgrimage to pray to be made well, and many believed they were cured by a miracle. Some people went to say they were sorry for crimes or sins they had committed. Other people just treated it as a holiday. Rome and Jerusalem were the most popular places to go. Pilgrims liked to buy a special badge to show where they had been. This badge came from the shrine of St Thomas Becket in Canterbury.

IT'S A MIRACLE
Stories of miracles were told about many good, holy people. This one is about a monk called Ailred. Ailred met a man who had swallowed a frog. The man was in great pain and his body was so swollen that he looked terrifying. All Ailred had to do was speak. The frog hopped out and sat on his hand, and the man got better at once.

· H O W · IMPORTANT · W A S · RELIGION?

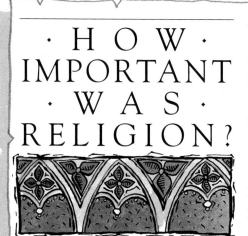

The Christian religion was extremely important to medieval people. Their faith in God gave meaning and purpose to their lives. Christianity also promised life after death to believers. For some people, religion was so important that they wanted to spend all their time praying and praising God. These people chose to become monks and nuns. Monks and nuns gave up everyday life to live in religious communities called monasteries and nunneries. These could be quite large, with their own church, hospital and farms to grow food.

ARCHITECTURE

The picture on the right shows part of the buildings used by the monks at Gloucester Abbey. Some religious houses were very plain or very poor. Others, like this one, used the best builders and the finest materials, because they wanted everything to add to the praise of God. But however simple or elaborate, all monasteries were laid out in a similar way, with the same basic buildings. They all had a church for worship, buildings for the monks or nuns to live in, workshops where everything they needed was made and a cloister, or enclosed courtyard, for the monks or nuns to walk around, or just to sit and think.

NUNS SINGING

These nuns are praising God in the church of their nunnery. As you can see, they are reading from service books. This made them very unusual, as hardly any medieval women could read. Some of the women who gave their lives to Christ by becoming nuns were famous for their wisdom and holiness. One of these was a woman called Julian of Norwich (1342–1416), who lived as a hermit. She had special visions of Christ, which were written down. Books of her thoughts on religion are still read today, and people interested in all sorts of questions about life find them very helpful.

GETTING THE TONSURE

A person who wanted to give his or her life to God had to do several things to show this. Monks had the top of their head shaved bare. This was called the 'tonsure'. The picture shows the ceremony where this was done. Monks and nuns also took vows promising to be obedient, to live as poor people and not to marry.

RICH GIFTS

Monks and nuns had a set daily timetable of prayer, with services at intervals all day and all night, every day of the year. People outside liked to know that this was going on, even though they couldn't join in. They gave gifts, like this richly decorated cross and chalice, to the monks and nuns, as a sign that they too wanted to praise God.

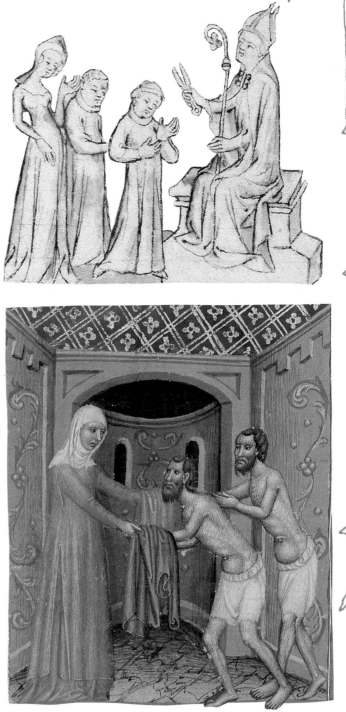

Crucifix

Chalice

MONASTERY TIMETABLE

Midnight until dawn:	services called Matins, Lauds and Prime
Morning:	monastery business, services called Tierce and Mass, work in the fields or gardens and indoors
Afternoon:	services called Sext and Nones, reading and other work
Evening:	services called Vespers and Compline

HELPING OTHERS

Monks and nuns were well known for helping others. Many religious communities had hospitals, where sick people were looked after, and special guest rooms, where travelers were welcomed. Poor people were given food and clothing, as you can see here. The Franciscans, a religious group founded by St Francis of Assisi (1181–1226) were especially loved for their kindness. But not all monks and nuns lived up to these high ideals – some were famous for being rich and greedy.

DID·PEOPLE ·GO·TO·THE· DOCTOR ?

When medieval people were sick, there were all sorts of people they could turn to for help, but very few of them were like modern doctors. There were doctors, but they were only really used by rich people. In towns, people went to see men called apothecaries, who mixed and sold medicines. They used many different ingredients – herbs, spices, metals, even insects such as crickets. Country folk made their own cures, or went to a local 'wise woman'.

WISE WOMAN

The picture shows a wise woman meeting a patient. Women like this knew a lot about illness and used cures that had been handed down from one generation to another. They made medicines out of natural ingredients such as fennel, chives and ivy. Some wise women also tried using magic to cure people. The medieval artist who drew this picture must have thought that wise women used magic, because he put little imps in his drawing. Priests often told people not to say spells and magic charms to sick people. Wise women were also often asked for potions and powders to make people fall in love or become beautiful. These were made out of all sorts of ingredients, from lettuce seeds to swans' feet.

DOCTOR AT WORK

Here, a doctor pulls an arrowhead out of his patient. Operations were often carried out by 'barber surgeons' – men whose main job was as a barber. Patients were knocked out with a big dose of wine, juice from opium poppies or other strong drugs. Afterwards they might be 'bled' by leeches, which sucked out blood that was thought to be diseased.

PRESCRIPTION PRAYER

Plague was a dreaded disease in the Middle Ages. There was no cure – all people could do was sniff sweet-smelling herbs and flowers in the hope that this would protect them. During outbreaks of plague, many people joined in religious processions to ask God to save them. The Church was sure that prayer could bring about miracle cures.

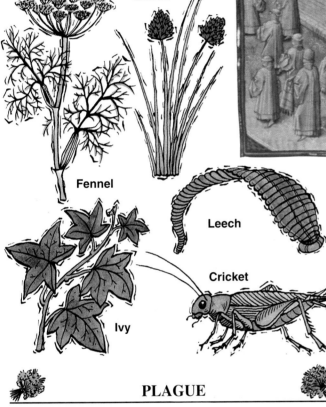

Chives

Fennel

Leech

Cricket

Ivy

MEDIEVAL PAIN RELIEF

The picture below shows people gathering herbs for cures like these. For a headache, take the roots of a peony and mix with oil of roses. Take a strip of linen cloth and soak it in the mixture. Then hold the wet linen to the patient's head. For toothache, take oil, sulphur and vinegar and mix them together. The patient should hold this mixture in his mouth.

PLAGUE

Plague came to Europe in 1347, when a ship arrived at Messina, in southern Italy, from the east. The ship's crew was dying of plague. A writer who heard about them wrote: 'In their bones they had so strong a disease that anyone even speaking to them was attacked by a death-dealing illness, and was bound to die.' Gradually, the plague traveled north through Italy and France, reaching England in 1348. Around half the population of Europe died; these are the figures for three cities:

In Florence, 100,000 out of 130,000 people died

In Norwich, 57,374 out of 70,000 people died

In Vienna, between 500 and 700 people died every day

In the Middle Ages people were ruled by kings, queens and nobles such as dukes, counts and countesses. These important people had one very special thing in common: they owned lots of land – far more than they needed to live on. Owning land gave people power, because they could rent it out to other people in return for service. Kings and queens let nobles have land in return for support and help in time of war. The nobles did the same with knights. The knights kept some land for themselves and let the rest out to peasant farmers in return for farm produce, money and work in the fields. This way of ruling a country is called 'feudalism'.

SUPPORT FOR THE LAW
Here, King Charles VII of France (1403–61) sits down in court to make sure his laws are being kept. Kings and queens in many countries had to struggle to make sure their rule was obeyed. They badly needed support from nobles and knights. Most nobles would support only men as rulers. In France, for example, a law stopped women ruling at all.

ROYAL POWER
Crowning a king or queen was a very great occasion. Some kings, such as those in France and England, were very powerful in the Middle Ages. But in eastern countries, like Poland and Hungary, kings were not much more important than the nobles.

Crown of Hungary

IN THE STOCKS
Making law-breakers feel embarrassed was a typical medieval punishment. Here, a monk and nun who have broken their religious vows have been put in the 'stocks' – a wooden punishment seat. Passers-by would laugh at them and throw cabbage leaves, rotten eggs and other kinds of trash.

ESCAPING JUSTICE
On the right is the great 'sanctuary' door knocker from Durham Cathedral. Criminals could escape the law by claiming 'sanctuary' – knocking on a church door and asking to be let in. They were allowed to stay inside for up to 40 days. After that they had to run away from the king's men, or if they promised to leave the kingdom for ever they would be taken to the coast and put on a ship.

Durham Cathedral sanctuary knocker

THE KING'S CASTLES
Guarding the king's castles was one of the important jobs that knights and nobles did. What they had to do was written down, so that there was no room for argument. Arrangements were made in special letters like this one sent by King Edward III of England (1312–77): 'The King to Sir Thomas de Rokeby, greetings. You will look after the castle at Edinburgh from this Easter until St John the Baptist's Day next year. You will guard it with 100 soldiers and 120 archers on horseback in peace time. If war breaks out, keep 140 soldiers and 160 archers on horseback there.'

RULING THE COUNTRYSIDE
The land was divided into large areas called estates. The estates were then divided into smaller farms, called manors. The person who ruled a manor was called the lord or lady of the manor. Here, peasants cut corn for the lord of the manor at harvest time. One of the lord's officials is telling them what to do.

In the Middle Ages there were people who painted pictures and made sculptures, stained glass, tapestry and other beautiful objects. But they didn't think of themselves as 'artists', just as workers, and they wanted to make their work as fine as possible as a way of serving God. Works of art were sometimes made for wealthy people's homes, but most often to decorate churches or to be used in church services. Often, well-to-do people paid for these works of art to show how religious they were.

RELIQUARY
This jeweled statue was made for a church in France, to keep the relics of a saint in. Relics were often a saint's bones and were very precious.

PAINTER AT WORK
Here, a woman painter works on a picture of the Virgin Mary with the baby Jesus, while a boy apprentice mixes paints. Art materials such as paints and brushes were all made by hand. You can see a box of brushes and some little seashells, used to hold paints, on the table in front. Most medieval artists didn't work by themselves, but in teams, like this pair. Often they did not put their names on their work, partly because it was such a team effort, so nobody now knows who they were.

ARTISTS' AIMS

Artists often chose to paint religious subjects, such as Christ and the saints, and this picture is a good example. It shows St Ninian, who helped to bring Christianity to Scotland after the fall of the Roman Empire. Around the edge are flowers that have been drawn in a very realistic way. This was part of an artistic revolution, as until late in the Middle Ages artists did not aim for a life-like look.

SCULPTURE

There was a lot of stone carving like this in medieval churches, but sculpture wasn't seen as a separate job. Many of the masons who worked on churches were able to turn their hand to all sorts of work – from routine building work to sculpting figures and special decorations in stone.

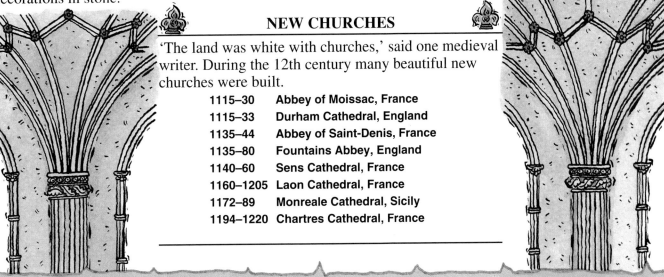

NEW CHURCHES

'The land was white with churches,' said one medieval writer. During the 12th century many beautiful new churches were built.

1115–30	**Abbey of Moissac, France**
1115–33	**Durham Cathedral, England**
1135–44	**Abbey of Saint-Denis, France**
1135–80	**Fountains Abbey, England**
1140–60	**Sens Cathedral, France**
1160–1205	**Laon Cathedral, France**
1172–89	**Monreale Cathedral, Sicily**
1194–1220	**Chartres Cathedral, France**

· W E R E · · T H E R E · SCIENTISTS · A N D · INVENTORS?

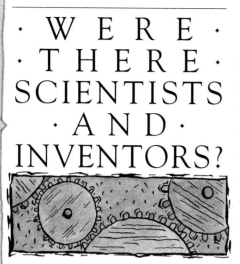

Some medieval people were interested in science and inventions, and arithmetic, geometry and astronomy were taught at university. But only a few people studied these subjects. Instead, most Christians were far more interested in studying God. In the Muslim Arab world, science was taken more seriously, and from the 1100s onwards this interest began to spread to Europe. By our standards, medieval science included some strange ideas – for example, people believed that everything was made out of earth, water, air and fire.

ASTRONOMER
On the right is a stone carving of an astronomer – someone who studies the planets and stars. Medieval scientists worked out that the earth was round, not flat, but there were many things they didn't know. Many medieval ideas, even scientific ones, were influenced by the Bible, for example the idea that the earth was the center of the universe. Later scientists showed this was wrong.

ASTROLABE
This is an astrolabe, which was used to measure the position of the stars in the sky. This information helped sailors at sea to work out where they were. Many of the first astrolabes were made by Arabs, because they had studied the stars very carefully. Gradually, during the Middle Ages, Christians in Europe began to learn this knowledge from the Arabs. Today, Arabic words are still used by astronomers: the star name 'Aldebaran' comes from Arabic.

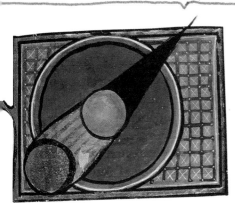

ECLIPSE

This is a medieval painting of an eclipse (the sun being hidden by the moon). People had many superstitious ideas about the stars and planets, as well as scientific ones. Dramatic events like eclipses were often seen as signs from God that people had done something wrong and that disasters would soon happen. Many educated people believed that the stars had a direct influence on their lives. This is called astrology.

WINDMILL

Windmills like this one were used to grind corn into flour. Many windmills were built in Europe from about 1100 onwards. Science in the Middle Ages was often very practical, and technology often used natural power, such as wind or water.

Windmill

MEDIEVAL 'INVENTIONS'

*c.*1100	Magnetic compass used by sailors
*c.*1100	Fly wheel – used to help control the speed of a machine
*c.*1180	Flying buttress – used to support the walls of large churches
*c.*1200	Treadle – a lever moved by the foot to make a machine work
*c.*1250	Pole lathe – used to spin pieces of wood around so a craftsman could carve them with both his hands
*c.*1270	Mechanical clock
*c.*1280	Spectacles
*c.*1280	Spinning wheel
*c.*1400	Crank – an arm (turning round-and-round movement into an up-and-down movement) used to help power a machine

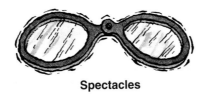

Spectacles

BELLS

This picture shows a man ringing church bells. Churches and monasteries needed bells to call people to prayer. They were also used to tell people of danger, such as a fire. The first metal bells in Europe were made in about AD800. Skilled metal-working techniques were needed in case the huge bells cracked as the hot liquid metal cooled down.

DID·PEOPLE ·TRAVEL?·

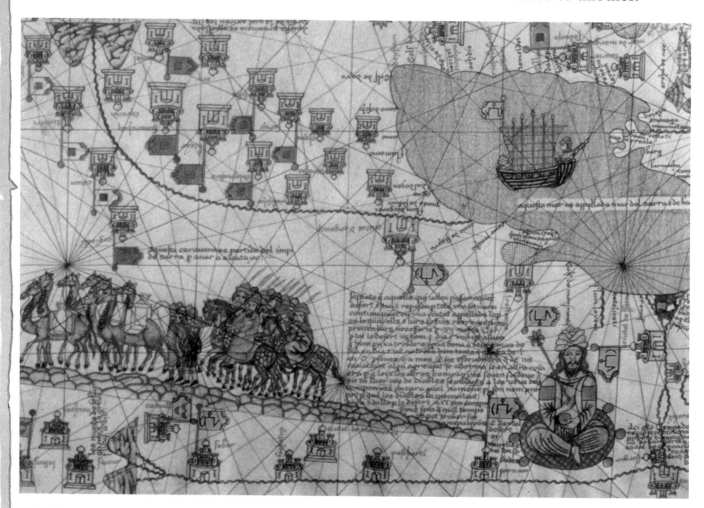

Most medieval people traveled very little. It was quite usual to live close to the place you were born for your whole life, especially if you were a peasant. Villeins were forbidden by law to move away from where they lived, but knights and rich people traveled more. Knights went to war and on Crusade (see page 43). They also took their families on visits to friends and relations, and moved around from one of their houses to another.

BEGINNING TO EXPLORE

In the Middle Ages, European merchants began to travel further from home to buy and sell goods. This map of Asia dates from 1375. By this time, people in Europe had begun to learn a little about Asia.
A famous merchant from Italy, Marco Polo (1254–1324) wrote an account of his travels there. He described the Mongol empire of Emperor Kublai Khan and its capital Khan-Balik (Beijing in modern China). Polo was very impressed by the Mongols' wealth and said that Khan-Balik did more trade than any other city in the world.

SLOW COACH!

Travel was very slow. These were maximum speeds:

Good horse and rider	15 miles per hour
Convoy of packhorses carrying merchants' goods	15 miles per day
Ships at sea	75–80 miles per day

But a good horse and rider couldn't ride at night, and ships might have to stay in port for days because of rough seas and bad weather.

TAKING TO THE SEAS

Going by boat was one of the easiest ways to travel, but, once at sea, sailors had to work out where to go. Ships often followed the coastline, to avoid getting lost in open water. Sailors navigated by the stars. From about 1100 onwards they used a magnetic compass to help them find north, as you can see in the picture on the left.

Cinnamon

Ginger

Cloves

SPICES

Spices from India and the east were very popular and very expensive. At first, European merchants had to buy spices from Arabs in the Middle East, who charged high prices. Later, the Europeans realized they could save money by traveling further east and dealing directly with the countries where the spices grew.

Mace

Nutmeg

PEDDLERS

Traveling salesmen like the one below were called peddlers. They went from village to village selling ribbons, candy and all sorts of treats. They traveled on foot, with all their goods packed on their back.

Like all travelers, they carried a big stick to lean on and to use if they were attacked by thieves on the way.

LUXURY TRAVEL

People traveled on foot, on horseback, or, if they were very rich, in luxurious covered wagons like this one. Even then travel was uncomfortable, as roads were muddy and full of pot holes.

WHAT·WAS·LIFE·LIKE·FOR SOLDIERS?

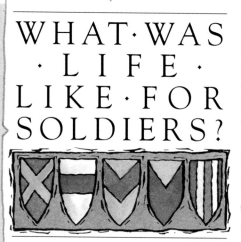

Medieval people were quick to use weapons when they quarrled, whether they were peasants or kings. When kings argued, they went to war, helped by the nobles and knights who supported them. When William of Normandy fought the battle of Hastings in 1066 and won control of England, he had 7,000 soldiers with him. Sometimes nobles fought each other for power, too. Struggles like this could mean civil war, splitting the country in two. Knights were the most important soldiers, but other sorts of soldiers, such as archers, fought alongside the knights on foot.

CASTLE FACTS

*c.*990	The first castles – a rectangular tower
*c.*1000	Motte and bailey castle – a wooden tower on an earth mound, surrounded by a ditch
*c.*1100	Shell keep – a stone wall round the top of the earth mound
1100s	Stone 'curtain walls' round the whole enclosure. Round towers instead of rectangular ones
*c.*1200	Extra towers added to the curtain walls
1200s	Concentric rings of walls built around the castle
*c.*1350	Gunpowder and cannons were used in battle to blow holes in castle walls

Castles were still built until about 1500, but gunpowder was the beginning of the end.

CASTLES

Kings and queens didn't keep a strong army all the time, as it was far too expensive. When war broke out, they called up all the knights and other soldiers who had promised to fight for them and sent them to attack enemy towns and castles. The people who designed castles were always trying new ways to make the castle defenses stronger, so that enemy soldiers would not be able to get inside. This castle, at Warkworth in Northumbria, has only one entrance – through the well-defended gatehouse. Enemy soldiers who tried to attack it would have had to cross the river and climb the steep bank and the high, strong walls. They would have been shot at by the defenders inside the towers, which had narrow windows to let arrows out but stop missiles coming through the other way. Often, the attackers didn't try to get in – they just sat outside waiting for the defenders to run out of food. This was called a siege.

CRUSADERS

Here King Louis IX of France (1215–70) sets out on Crusade with his knights. Crusades were 'holy' wars, fought by armies from Christian Europe against the Arabs who controlled the Middle East. The Middle East was very important to both sides for religious reasons, and it was called the 'Holy Land' because of this. The Crusaders won control of Jerusalem from the Arabs, but lost it again in 1187 to the great Arab leader, Saladin (1138–93).

Sword

WEAPONS

The knight's most important weapons were his sword and his lance. Jewels and even holy relics were set into swords, but lances were just long shafts of wood, which often shattered in battle. Grenades, like the ones below, were invented during the Middle Ages. They were clay pots, full of an inflammable liquid called naphtha.

Grenades

BOWMAN

At the end of the Middle Ages bowmen like this became more important in battle than knights, because they could use their bows to kill people from a long range. There were two different kinds of bow: the crossbow (like this one) and the longbow.

ARMOR

This knight is wearing protective chain mail armor, made of flexible metal loops. Later, knights wore armor made out of metal plates, which was heavy and very difficult to move in. Knights in armor who fell off their horses were unable to run away.

·GLOSSARY·

APOTHECARY A person who mixed medicines and often also acted as a doctor.

APPRENTICE A child who was learning a craft or trade by helping an adult do his or her job. The apprentice's parents usually had to pay for this training, which lasted about seven years.

CASTLE A house and a fort rolled into one. Knights lived in castles. But castles were also key points in battles and war, so they had to have strong defenses – good walls, towers and other barriers, so an enemy couldn't get in.

CHALICE A special drinking cup used at religious services in the Christian Church.

CRUSADE A holy war fought by Christians against Muslims in the Middle East.

FEUDAL SYSTEM The system of ruling the country in the Middle Ages, through which people were rented land in exchange for doing services (e.g. fighting or growing food) for their landlord.

FRIAR A Christian man who gave his life to God by taking special religious vows. There were two main groups of friars: the Franciscans, founded by St Francis of Assisi, and the Dominicans, founded by St Dominic.

GUILD A club for traders doing similar jobs in a town. Guilds made rules about quality and prices, and also held feasts and processions.

HARROWING Breaking up the soil using a tool with many prongs, pulled by horses or oxen.

HERMIT A man or woman who lived alone and spent all his or her time praying and praising God.

KNIGHT An important medieval soldier. Knights fought on horseback. They were important rulers as well.

MANOR A farm in the country, belonging to an important person such as a knight. The land on most manors was divided up so that some fields were kept for the person who owned the manor, and some were let out to peasants.

MERCHANT Someone who made a living by buying and selling things. Many merchants became rich by trading with different countries, like the merchants who bought spices from the east and sold them to customers in Western Europe.

MIRACLE A surprising happening which people who believe in God think is brought about by His power. Examples of miracles include people suddenly being cured of an illness or weakness.

MONK A man who gave his life to God by taking special religious vows. Monks lived together in groups in religious houses called monasteries.

NOBLE A very important person, who controlled a great deal of land and ruled large numbers of people. Nobles usually had titles, such as duke, count etc.

NUN A woman who gave her life to God by taking special religious vows. Nuns lived together in groups in religious houses called nunneries.

PARCHMENT Animal skin used for writing on. Sheep's skin and goat's skin were widely used.

PEASANT A poor country person who lived by farming.

PILGRIMAGE A journey taken for religious reasons. Pilgrimages were usually made to churches which had special links with holy men and women. People who went on pilgrimage were called pilgrims.

POPE The leader of the Christian Church in Western Europe.

PRIEST A Christian leader in charge of a church.

RELIC Something to remember a saint or holy person by. A relic could be almost anything which had touched the saint when he or she was alive, such as a piece of his or her clothing. When the saint was dead, parts of his or her body, such as fingernails, pieces of bone or locks of hair, might become a relic.

SAINT Someone who leads a specially good and holy life, like St Francis of Assisi.

SHRINE The place where a saint is buried.

THRESHING Beating harvested crops (e.g. corn or wheat) to separate out the grain.

TOURNAMENT A competition between two knights on horseback.

VILLEIN A peasant who had no rights at all. He or she couldn't move away from where they lived, couldn't get married and couldn't educate their children without permission.

· I N D E X ·

abacus 21
angels 8
animals 9, 13, 14, 24
apothecaries 32, 44
apprentices 17, 25, 44
Arabs 38, 41, 43
architecture 30
armor 43
art 36–7
astrolabes 38
astronomy 38

banquets 15
bears, dancing 24
bells 39
Bernardino, St 28
Bible 20, 38
bishops 28
books 11, 20, 30
bowmen 43

castles 9, 10, 18, 22, 23, 24, 27, 35, 42, 44
cathedrals 10, 20, 22, 28, 35, 37
Charles VII, King of France 34
children 12, 13, 16–17
Chrétien de Troyes 10, 11
Christians 8, 10, 11, 20, 28–31, 38, 44
Christmas 24, 25
Church 10, 11, 15, 20, 25, 28–9, 33, 44
churches 10, 30, 35, 36, 37, 39,
clothes 26–7
coins 22
craftsworkers 17, 18, 22, 23
Crusades 10, 11, 40, 43, 44

Dante Alighieri 11
diseases 11, 19, 32–3
doctors 32, 44

Easter 12, 24
eclipse 39
estates 35

fairs 11, 24
families 16–17, 40
farming 9, 12–13, 30, 34, 35, 44
Feudal System 12, 34, 44
fish 12
food 12–15, 30, 31
Francis of Assisi, St 11, 31, 44
Franciscans 11, 31, 44
furniture 18, 19

God 8, 22, 28, 29, 30, 31, 33, 36, 38, 44
golf 25
guilds 23, 44

harvests 13, 35, 44
Henry IV, King of England 15
herbs 14, 33
hermits 27, 44
holidays 24–5
horses 13, 23, 40, 41, 43, 44
hospitals 31
houses 18–19
hunting 13, 24

inventions 38–9

Jesus Christ 25, 29, 36, 37
Jews 11, 28
Julian of Norwich, St 30

kings 11, 14, 22, 23, 28, 29, 34, 35, 42
knights 11, 14, 16, 18, 22, 23, 26, 27, 34, 35, 40, 42, 43, 44

landowners 12, 34, 44
Latin language 11, 20, 21, 28
laws 9, 34, 35, 40

manors 35, 44
maps 9, 40
masons 22, 27, 37
May Day 25
merchants 11, 18, 20, 22, 23, 40, 41, 44
miracles 29, 44
monasteries 18, 20, 28, 30, 31, 39, 44
money 22
Mongols 11, 40
monks 10, 15, 18, 20, 22, 25, 29, 30, 31, 35, 44
music 24, 25, 30
Muslims 10, 28, 38, 44

nobles 11, 16, 22, 24, 26, 27, 29, 34, 35, 42, 44
nunneries 18, 30, 44
nuns 18, 22, 25, 27, 30, 31, 35, 44

oxen 13, 44

parchment 20, 44
Paston, John 16

peasants 8, 9, 12, 23, 14, 15, 17, 18, 19, 22, 26, 34, 35, 40, 42, 44
pedlars 41
pigs 14
pilgrimages 29, 44
plague 11, 33
poetry 11
Polo, Marco 11, 40
prayers 20, 22, 28, 31, 39, 44
priests 20, 28, 32, 44
punishments 29, 35

queens 14, 22, 28, 34, 42

rats 19
relics 36, 43, 44
religion 10, 28–31
Richard II, King of England 8
Roman Empire 8, 11, 37

saints 8, 29, 36, 37, 44
schools 20–1
science 38–9
sculpture 37
seals 21
servants 16, 18, 21
ships 40, 41
soldiers 11, 16, 42–3
spices 41, 44
stained glass 10, 29, 36

tonsure 31
tournaments 23, 44
towns 9, 11, 17, 18, 19, 23
toys 16
trade 11, 41
travel 40-1

universities 10, 21

villages 11, 28, 41
villeins 8, 40, 44

wars 11, 42–3, 44
weapons 16, 42, 43
weaving 23
William of Normandy 10, 42
windmills 39
wine 12
women 17, 22, 23, 24, 26, 27, 30, 32, 34
work 22–3
writing 20